The
Forest

In the clearing

From his observation tower, the forester can watch the forest animals in the clearing. The clearing is a meadow in the forest on which no trees grow.

Here, where the sunbeams shine right down to the ground, many flowers and types of grass grow. They taste good to the deer and other wildlife. Up in the sky, a buzzard is keeping watch for a nice tasty mouse. Butterflies and other insects fly from flower to flower.

buzzard

wild boar

deer

metalmarks

? Look and learn!

A fawn has hidden itself in the big picture. Can you find it?

Which animal is casting this shadow? Can you find it in the picture? What is it watching out for?

forester in
observation tower

Wild boar

A pack of wild boar are rummaging around in the mud for roots and worms. There are young boar among them. They have a light stripy coat. This enables them to hide well in the grass. Their mother keeps an eye on them. The hunter calls the mother a wild sow, and the father with his powerful tusks a tusker.

roe deer

Butterflies are insects. Many
of them have beautifully
coloured wings!

swallow-tail

blue butterfly

cockchafer

green lacewing

On the forest floor

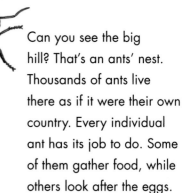

The forest floor is a living world. Take a closer look! Beetles, woodlice, ants and centipedes scurry around. Spiders lie in wait for their prey. Earthworms eat the fallen leaves and turn it into fertile soil.

All plants take root in the forest floor: big, strong trees, low shrubs, slender grasses and flowers.

Can you see the big hill? That's an ants' nest. Thousands of ants live there as if it were their own country. Every individual ant has its job to do. Some of them gather food, while others look after the eggs.

Earthworms burrow through the ground. It's dangerous for them on the surface: many animals like to eat them!

The grass frog feels very comfortable on the damp forest floor. It's looking out for insects.

centipede

In the ground, you can also find many larvae. They pupate and then, as fully-grown insects, out they slide.

Mushrooms have a stem and a cap. They are attached to the forest floor by a web of white threads.

Several mushrooms, like this fly agaric, are poisonous. You mustn't eat them!

Lichens are mixed creatures, half mushroom and half algae. They grow as crust on stones or the bark of trees.

Mosses grow as soft, green pillows where it is dark and damp.

salamander

moss

lichen

pseudo-scorpion

wolf spider

woodlice

What kind of tree is that?

In the forest, both deciduous and coniferous trees grow. You can easily tell the difference between them.

Deciduous trees are green only in the summer. In the autumn, the leaves change colour and fall. In the winter the trees are bare.

Coniferous trees are green all year round. They include spruce, fir and pine trees.

pine needles

pine cones

pine

Pine cones are small and round.

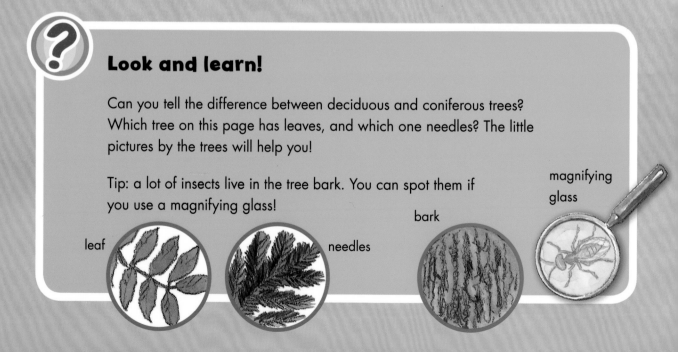

Look and learn!

Can you tell the difference between deciduous and coniferous trees? Which tree on this page has leaves, and which one needles? The little pictures by the trees will help you!

Tip: a lot of insects live in the tree bark. You can spot them if you use a magnifying glass!

leaf

needles

bark

magnifying glass

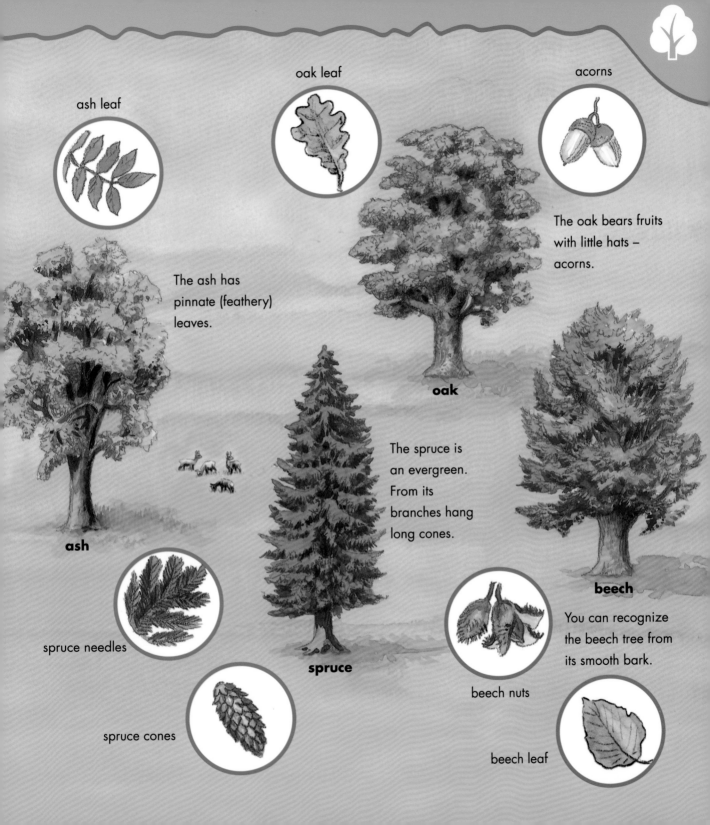

ash leaf

oak leaf

acorns

The oak bears fruits with little hats – acorns.

The ash has pinnate (feathery) leaves.

oak

The spruce is an evergreen. From its branches hang long cones.

ash

beech

spruce needles

You can recognize the beech tree from its smooth bark.

beech nuts

spruce

spruce cones

beech leaf

Chirping in the forest

In the forest, you can hear the birds chirping. Songbirds are especially good at warbling! The birds live in the trees and build their nests there. They mainly feed their young on insects.

Many types of bird fly to warmer regions of the earth in the autumn. They spend the winter there. They are called migratory birds. Other types of bird stay here all year round. They are less bothered by the cold.

A tit incubating eggs

In many places, the forester hangs up nesting boxes. There, the birds can incubate and raise their young in safety.

Know your birds!

Many birds, like the nightingale, chirp really beautifully. But even they have first to learn how to sing! Do you know what these birds are called?

Where is this swarm of birds heading?

The woodpecker has a very hard beak. It uses this beak to peck away at the bark, where it finds many insects. For its young, it pecks out a hole in the trunk for a nest.

cuckoo

great spotted woodpecker

These young tits are just learning how to fly – they are becoming fully fledged.

tree pipit

young cuckoo

The cuckoo lays its eggs in the nests of other birds. There, its young are incubated and fed by other parents.

Birds have their enemies, too. Here, a stone marten has discovered the chicks of a nuthatch in their nest.

Tree bark rubbing

Place a sheet of white paper onto the trunk of a tree and rub over it with a soft pencil. That way, you can transfer the structure of the bark onto the paper. Can you see that the bark of each type of tree looks different?

Mouse bones

Owls and screech owls eat their prey with its skin and hair still on. They regurgitate as pellets anything that they are unable to digest. If you find one of these pellets, drop it in some water. Then the little mouse bones will become visible.

Explorers in the forest!

Only at first sight does the forest seem empty and uninhabited. Take a closer look, and you'll make a few discoveries! There are simple tools to help you explore.

Many forest dwellers are very small. You need to take a very close look to spot them! Others are timid, and hide well away in daylight. For that reason, you need to be really quiet if you want to see or hear them!

What's that rustling noise? It's a mouse looking for food. If you keep very quiet, you'll hear it!

mite

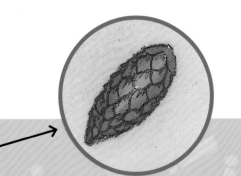

Seed protection

Dry spruce cones are open to let the seeds fall out. In water they close up so that the seeds won't go rotten. You can observe this if you put a spruce cone into a glass of water.

A trick with the magnifying glass

With a magnifying glass you can also see really small forest dwellers like this mite.

Night in the forest

At dusk, things become very lively in the forest. Deer, stags and hares come out of their hiding places.

The vixen hunts after food for her young, in the protection of darkness. The polecat has caught a mouse. The bat flutters silently through the night.

Barn owls have a good sense of hearing. They also fly almost silently. So at night they turn into dangerous hunters.

fallow deer

hedgehog

? Prickly balls

Can you see the little hedgehog? It's just pulling an earthworm out of the ground.

What can it use to protect itself if it's attacked? What does it do if it is in danger?

The tawny owl can use its big eyes to see well and hunt even in the dark.

Bats utter high-pitched shrieks that human beings cannot hear. The echo of these shrieks helps them to find their way.

In their lair, the young foxes wait for their mother to return with food.

rowan

raspberry

The nimble polecat has a taste for frogs, birds, eggs and mice.

Seasons in the forest

Over the year, life in the forest changes. In spring, nature awakens: buds and leaves grow, and young animals are born.

In the summer, the forest is green and full of life. The animals gather food for the winter.

In the autumn, the leaves change colour and fall. Mushrooms grow. Migratory birds head south.

In the winter, the forest seems to be asleep. Deciduous trees are bare and leafless. Many animals hibernate. Others eat their store of food.

The dormouse hibernates. During this time, it does not eat. For that reason, it needs to find as much food as possible in the months before.

When snow has fallen, you can see and identify the tracks of animals especially clearly.

In the autumn, the leaves turn yellow and red. Now many kinds of fruit also turn ripe. You can spot them in the forest!

spruce cones

hazelnuts

barn owl

pine marten

squirrel

roe deer

stag beetle

salamander

In spring and summer, the forest is very lively. Now you can watch many animals.

Looking for tracks

A story to read aloud

Uncle Jack is a forester and looks after the forest and its creatures. Today, Luke is going to go with him! It's a fine, clear winter morning. Jack and Luke walk along the edge of the forest. It's quiet all around them.

Suddenly Jack hands Luke his binoculars and whispers, 'Look! Over there! Can you see the deer?' Luke can't see anything but blurry brown patches. 'You need to focus the binoculars!' says Uncle Jack and turns a little wheel on the binoculars. Now Luke can see the deer.

Through the binoculars, the deer seem as close as if they were standing right in front of him! Then one of them looks up and stares at him. At the next moment, all the deer run off into the forest. 'That's a shame!' says Luke, disappointed. 'Why have they run off?' 'Deer don't see very well, so they have a better sense of smell and hearing. They sensed our presence.'

Now the two are climbing the observation tower. From so high up, you have a good view! 'You can see so much from up here!' says Uncle Jack, pointing to a spot on the edge of the forest. 'But there's nothing there – not a single animal!' says Luke in surprise. 'You'll see. Come with me!' smiles his uncle.

In the clearing, Luke takes a good look round. All is quiet, nothing moves. 'Most animals hide during the daytime. But you can find their tracks!' explains Uncle Jack. 'Do you see the hole under the tree? That's the entrance to a badger's sett. Down inside, the badger waits until nightfall, when it can come out. The sett can go down over fifteen feet!' 'So have you ever seen a badger?' asks Luke in excitement. 'Yes, at night time. But, of course, you need to be lucky. Badgers are very shy creatures.'

'Why does the tree next to it not have any bark? Was that the badger?' asks Luke curiously. 'Well observed! No, that was deer or stags. Now, in the winter time, animals can't find so much food. So sometimes, unfortunately, they also eat the bark off the trees. We feed them so that they cause less damage.'

Luke nods. Now he knows: if you take a closer look in the forest, there is a lot to discover! He is already looking forward to his next walk through the forest with Uncle Jack.

Who works in the forest?

So that the forest will stay healthy, and the trees will not be attacked by pests, it needs to be maintained. The forester and other forest workers do this job. They also make sure that the forest animals remain healthy, and that in every season they can find enough to eat.

Many trees need to be felled, because they are diseased. Others are felled because furniture can be made out of their wood, or because they can be processed into paper.

As they work, the foresters try to take as much care as they can not to disturb the shy forest creatures.

Here a tree is being felled. The woodcutter separates the branches from the trunk with a power saw.

red deer

In the winter, deer and stags cannot always find enough to eat. Then the forester gives them extra food.

power saw

bark stripper

So that the newly-planted trees can grow properly, the forest worker cuts down the undergrowth with a knife.

young forest

The forest worker strips the bark from the fallen tree trunks with a machine.

This forest worker is protecting the bark from hungry deer with a wire mesh.

wire mesh

Forest animals and human beings

Over the years, human beings have cut down more and more forests. They have replaced them with fields, and built houses and cities. In this way, the area in which forest animals can live is becoming smaller all the time.

Some forest animals are threatened by extinction. They have become rare. Others have grown used to humans and have followed them into their cities and residential areas. They now live here and go hunting for food mainly at night-time.

The blackbird used to be a very shy forest bird. Now you often see them in the garden.

The lynx is the largest European predatory cat. It was so intensively hunted that it almost died out. For that reason, specially bred lynxes are put out in forests, where they are protected.

Wild boar rummage for food in city parks and gardens!